Nugget Series

Momma Says

Book 1

Flo McLain, RN

ISBN 978-1-64258-559-9 (paperback)
ISBN 978-1-64258-560-5 (digital)

Christian Faith Publishing, Inc.
832 Park Avenue
Meadville, PA 16335
www.christianfaithpublishing.com

Printed in the United States of America

To my mom, Mary Elizabeth Hancock.

Author's Note

Nuggets of spiritual wisdom for children ages 2 through 7. Designed for parental readings.

Story No. 1

First Things First

Johnny scratched his red head, waking with a big yawn. His first thought was of his new red bike.

"I can't wait to get outside," he whispered to himself.

In his hazy daydreaming, he could hear his mother's voice calling, "Johnny, Johnny, rise and shine!"

Jumping out of bed, he ran down the steps, yelling, "*Zoom … Zoom … Zoom*!"

"Look, Mom, I'm so fast! Can I ride my bike now? Please … pl … ea … se …," he begged.

"Wow! Slow down, Johnny. Remember, *first things first*. Sit down and eat your breakfast. You need to gas up your engine with food."

"Oh yeah, I forgot."

Johnny rushed through his breakfast.

"I'm done. Can I go outside now Mom, please?"

"In your pajamas? Hey, did you forget *first things first*, Johnny?"

"Oh yeah, I forgot."

He ran to his room, flying to get his clothes and shoes on.

"I'm ready, Mom. Can I go out now, please?"

"Johnny, Johnny, did you forget your teeth. *First things first*, honey."

"Do I have to, Mom?"

She smiled. "You bet!"

He brushed his teeth as fast as he could. Showing his mom his teeth, he headed for the door.

"Johnny," he heard his mother's voice call. "You forgot the most important thing of all!"

He froze in his tracks. He peeked over his shoulder, and his mother was grinning and holding her arms wide open.

"My hug!"

He ran to her arms and squeezed her tightly as she whispered into his ear, *"First things first*, sweetie. Love ya!"

The End

Story No. 2

Easy Does It

Emily peeked out her window. She saw Johnny outside on his new red bike.

How does he do that? she thought as she watched him speeding up and down his long, circular driveway. She rubbed her bandaged knee, the knee she fell on trying to learn to ride her own new pink Princess Flyer.

"I just can't do it!" she cried.

She looked out her bedroom window again.

"Oh no! There's Bruce! He's even faster than Johnny!"

Bruce, the tallest kid on the block, could outride everybody on his Blue Blaster.

"It makes me so mad! I wish I was a boy so I could ride that fast," she mumbled to herself.

"Emily, where are you?" she heard her mother call

"I'm in my room, Mom."

Suddenly, her mother was standing in the doorway. "Aren't you going outside today, Emily?"

Emily didn't answer.

"It's a nice sunny, warm day, honey. I see Johnny and Bruce are outside with their new bikes, playing. Why don't you see if they will let you play with them?"

"I can't," Emily grunted.

"Why not?" asked her mom.

"'Cause, I can't!" Emily snapped.

"Okay, little girl, but you still need to go outside and get some fresh air. Come on now. Let's go."

Emily dragged her feet.

Once outside, there sat her pink Princess Flyer.

"I can't ride that thing, Mom," she complained.

"Emily, just keep trying and you'll get it. Remember *easy does it*."

Emily hopped on the shiny, silvery seat and began peddling. As the little bike picked up speed, she felt afraid. All of a sudden she was on the ground again!

She looked up and there was Johnny and Bruce next door, laughing at her.

"Emily, are you okay?" called her mom.

Emily was angry. She jumped up. She grabbed a long stick. She started hitting her bike with the stick till it broke.

"I hate you," she yelled at the pink Princess Flyer.

"Emily, *easy does it*! You're trying too hard. Let me help you," her mom said as she hugged her. "It will be okay. Let's practice together."

Her mom showed her how to hold the handle bars and peddle more slowly. She kept saying, "*Easy does it*, Emily. Take your time."

Emily kept trying, when all of a sudden she realized her mom wasn't holding onto the bike.

"I did it!" she shouted. "I did it!"

Johnny and Bruce and Emily played the rest of the day on their new bikes.

When Emily felt afraid she would just say to herself, "*Easy does it*!" and she was okay.

The End

Story No. 3

How Important Is It?

"Jacob, Jacob, where are you?" his mother called.

"Here I am, Mom, in the basement."

"Oh, there you are, Jacob. Guess what! Harry and his mother are coming over for lunch. Isn't that great?"

"Yeah …," replied Jacob. "I suppose so …"

"Why do you say it that way, Jacob?"

Jacob shrugged his shoulders.

"Could it be you don't like it when Harry plays with your stuff, especially the train set?"

"Yeah," he said rather sharply. "He always wants to be the driver!"

"Jacob, what's more important? The toy or Harry's feelings? After all he is your best friend. You need to share. *How important is it* to be the driver?"

"I like to drive, Mom!" he said firmly.

"I know, Jacob. But sharing, taking turns, is what's important. Just try, okay?"

"Okay, okay!" he snapped

Harry and his mother, Jane, arrived in a flurry. Harry and Jacob immediately headed for the basement playroom.

"Hold on you guys … lunch first."

"Ah, Ma-a-a, do we have to?" whined Harry.

"Yes, you have to!" answered Harry's mother, Jane.

After gobbling down their sandwiches, off they flew down the steps to the playroom.

A short while later, Harry was crying. The moms ran downstairs to the playroom.

"What's going on, boys?" Jacob's mom asked.

"Jacob won't let me have a turn running the train," Harry cried.

"We already talked about this, Jacob. Okay, you have a choice—Harry or the train. Which do you choose to play with, Jacob?"

Jacob stared down at the floor. "I want to be the driver! It's my train!" he yelled

"Sorry, Jane," said Jacob's mother, Sarah, looking embarrassed.

"That's okay, Sarah, Harry and I have to go anyway. I have an errand to run. See you guys later. Maybe you'll be in a better mood next time we come, Jacob."

Several days passed by, and Jacob was almost always playing with his toy train set. But after a while Jacob grew bored playing all by himself.

"Mom, can you call Harry's mom so Harry can come over?"

"Don't you remember, you picked the train over Harry, your friend?"

"But I miss Harry, Mom."

"I'm sorry, son, that being the boss of the train was more important than Harry's feelings. But you did have a choice. Next time maybe you'll think about *how important is it* to always be first, to always win!

Jacob flopped down on the couch and stared at the floor. He was really sad.

About an hour later, the doorbell rang. Jacob heard his mom say, "Hi, Jane, how are you?"

Jacob ran to the kitchen. His face fell in disappointment when he saw Jane standing all alone.

"Where's Harry?" he questioned.

Just then a small puppy poked his nose through the door, dragging Harry behind him.

"Jacob, come outside with me and my new puppy, Blackie. Isn't he great?"

Jacob's eyes welled up with tears. "Can I, Mom?"

"Of course, Jacob. Isn't it nice that Harry is sharing his puppy with you? He knows *how important it is* to share with a friend and so do we. Right, Jacob?"

Both boys smiled happily at one another.

"You bet, Mom!"

The End

Story No. 4

Just for Today

Sister Agatha looked out over her gold-rimmed glasses at the room full of six-year-olds.

"Good morning, class" she chirped like a bird.

"Good morning, Sister Agatha," they mumbled back.

"Well, well, not too many smiling faces out there today."

The children squirmed in their seats uncomfortably.

"Class, what's it doing outside today?"

"Raining, Sister."

"That's right! There's no sunshine today, so *just for today* we have to make our own sunshine."

Emily raised her hand. "How do we do that, Sister?" she asked.

"Well now, I'm going to show you how. Rainy days make most people sad, and sunny days make most people happy. *Just for today*, even though it's rainy, we are going to choose to be sunny and happy. Okay, class, close your eyes and imagine a happy time or place you remember. It could be a picnic, a beach, your home, or playing with a puppy."

The children started to giggle with delight.

"That's good, class. Keep imagining your special place. When you are done, open your eyes. Does anyone want to share their sunny place?"

Johnny raised his hand, waving it back and forth insistently. "Me, Sister, me!"

"Okay, Johnny."

"My new bike makes me happy. I can fly like a bird on my bike!"

"Good, Johnny, very good. Okay, class, take out a piece of paper and draw me a picture of your sunny place. *Just for today* we choose to make our own sunshine and be happy."

The End

Story No. 5

Keep an Open Mind

"Mamma, Mamma, can you help me?"
Melissa's mother flew up the stairs.
"What is it, Melissa? What's wrong?"

Melissa, age five, was standing still outside her bedroom door with her hand outstretched.

Her mother looked down, and there in her hand was a white tooth!

"Well, well, Melissa! What have you got?"

"My tooth felt out, Mamma!"

"So I see." She smiled. "Don't worry, Melissa, a new one will grow in its place."

"What should I do with this tooth?" Melissa asked.

"Why put it under your pillow, of course!" her mother answered.

"Why?"

"So the tooth fairy will come."

"What's a tooth fairy, Mamma?"

"It's like a tiny elf with wings. It will take your tooth and leave money in its place!"

"I don't believe it, Mamma."

"Melissa, *keep an open mind*. Just because it's new and different doesn't mean it's not so. *Keep an open mind*, honey."

"Well, okay," Melissa answered.

That night Melissa did as her mom told her. She put the tooth under her pillow.

The next morning, Melissa could not wait to wake up to see if the tooth fairy had really come. She lifted her pillow up, and there, shining back at her, was a silver quarter and no tooth!

"Mamma, Mamma!" she screamed. "The tooth fairy came. Look!"

"That's great, Melissa! Good for you. See, it pays to *keep an open mind*."

The End

Story No. 6

Keep It Simple

Cassie sat on the couch, her arms folded, staring at her mother and older brother, Jacob. She was mad!

"Come on Cassie, put your diaper on so we can go to the playground to play," her mother asked.

"*No*," Cassie said firmly. "*No, no, no!*"

"Cassie, when I was two, I had to wear diapers too." Jacob said kindly.

"I want big-girl pants!" Cassie yelled.

"Cassie, you have to go on the potty before you can get big-girl pants," her mother said firmly. "We need to *keep it simple*! If you go potty, you get big-girl pants."

Cassie cried as her mother put her diaper and pants on.

That night, after supper, Cassie walked to the bathroom and stared at the potty chair. It was just her size.

Her mom noticed her staring and gently said, "*Keep it simple*, Cassie. Go potty and get pants."

Cassie really, really, really wanted to wear her new big-girl pants.

She tugged and tugged to get her diaper off and sat down on the potty … and she sat … and she sat … and she sat. A long … long … long time went by when all of a sudden she heard a sprinkle of tinkle hit the plastic pot of her potty chair.

She was amazed!

"Look at the yellow water, Momma!" she said.

"That's great, Cassie!" her mom cheered.

Cassie smiled. She was proud. Cassie thought, *I love my potty*.

The next day Cassie was so happy she got to wear her big-girl pants outside!

"Remember, Cassie, *keep it simple*! Go potty to be a big girl."

And she did.

The End

Story No. 7

Let Go and Let God

Emily was sad. Her kitty, Lu-lu-bell, was lying so still.

"Why isn't she moving, Mama?" Emily asked.

"Well, Emily, Lu-lu-bell is dead. She's gone to kitty heaven."

Emily cried. "But I don't want Lu-lu-bell to go away. I want her to stay here with me!"

"I know," her mom said. "But Lu-lu-bell was very old and very sick. *God* took Lu-lu-bell home to heaven to rest. You have to *let go and let God*."

Emily stamped her feet angrily. "No, no, I won't let go. I'm holding on to her. She's my kitty, not *God's*."

Emily's mom held her tightly and rocked her. "My poor Emily, I know you are sad, but don't you want Lu-lu-bell to be happy? Remember how she was limping and meowing? Lu-lu-bell's doctor said she was very sick and couldn't play anymore. But in heaven Lu-lu-bell will have no pain at all. She can play in *God's* house now that she is dead."

Emily frowned.

"We all belong to *God*, Emily. Lu-lu-bell was just visiting us for a while. Now *God* took her back home again to heaven. You have to *let go and let God* now, Emily."

"Will *God* let me visit her sometime?" Emily asked.

"Someday little one, someday."

"Okay, Mama. Bye-bye, Lu-lu-bell, I love you."

They wrapped Lu-lu-bell in Emily's favorite old baby blanket and placed her in a shoebox. Then they buried her behind the rose bushes. A big rock with her name marked the spot. Under her name, Mama wrote, "*Let go and let God.*"

The End

Story No. 8

Let It Begin with Me

Nicholas was six years old, and Crissie was five. They were brother and sister. Sometimes they would fight.

One day, Crissie couldn't find her brown teddy bear. She went into her brother's room, and there it sat on Nick's bed. She grabbed it and hid it under her bed.

Later that day, Nick called down the stairs to his mom. "Where's my teddy bear, Mom?"

"It's on your bed, Nick."

"No, it's not," he called back.

Crissie knew where his bear was, but she said nothing. Their mom came upstairs.

"Have you seen Nick's bear, Crissie?"

"No, Mom," Crissie said. She lied.

"Are you sure, Crissie?"

"Yeah."

Nick started to cry.

"I can't sleep without my bear, Mom!"

"Here, dear, come sleep with Mom. We'll look some more tomorrow."

Crissie felt guilty. She reached under the bed and grabbed what she had thought was her bear. She hugged the bear, hiding it under her covers.

The next morning Crissie awoke early. As her sleepy eyes opened, she saw the leg of a teddy bear sticking out between the dresser and the wall.

Oh no, she thought. *That's really my teddy bear!*

She rushed to hide Nick's bear under the bed again. She grabbed her own bear and climbed back into bed.

Just then her mom came to the door of her room. She sat on the side of Crissie's bed and hugged her. "Crissie, are you sure you didn't see Nick's bear?"

Crissie didn't say anything.

"You know, Crissie, sometimes we have to say we're sorry. When I make a mistake, like losing daddy's car keys the other day, well, I was the first to say I'm sorry. *I let it begin with me!* Then it was easier for Dad to forgive me."

Crissie was quiet for a long time. Then she reached under the bed and picked out Nick's bear.

"I see," said her mom. "Nick is in my bed, Crissie. Better to *let it begin with you*—saying you're sorry, that is!"

Crissie grabbed both bears and tiptoed into the bedroom. "Nick … Nick … look! I found your bear. Sorry, I lost it."

Nick rubbed his eyes. "Oh boy, thanks Crissie! That's okay, I forgive you."

The two bears and the two children jumped up and down on the bed.

The End

Story No. 9

Listen and Learn

Chadd was looking bored. He had played with all his video games and all his toys. All his friends were away. Nana, his grandmother, was there to babysit for the day.

"So, Chadd, what's up? How are you doing?" she asked.

"Nothin'." He shrugged his shoulders.

"Well then, we'll have to create something out of nothin'!"

"What do you mean?" he asked.

"*Listen and learn*, that's what I mean. Look around you at this kitchen. What do you see?"

"A table, chairs, stove, dishes—stuff like that," he answered.

"The key, Chadd, is to not just see the item but to think to yourself, *What can I do with these items to entertain myself?* For example, the table and chairs can easily be converted to a fort with a sheet and some imagination. The flour can be mixed with baking soda and water to make clay, etc. etc. The list is endless! I see a small recorder. Any ideas, Chadd?" she asked.

"No," he answered.

"Well, let's tape ten common noises. We'll give a hint on the tape, like say, 'This noise is essential in the kitchen.' Then we'll record the running faucet. When your parents come home, we'll test them to see if they can identify the sounds. We'll call the tape *listen and learn*."

Chadd grew excited. "Yeah, let me try it."

That whole afternoon was spent recording noises in and around the house.

Later that evening Chadd's parents came home. They were amused at the little contest.

The sounds Chadd chose ranged from the flushing of the toilet, which drew lots of laughs, to the whistling of the tea kettle. All in all, Chadd and Nana had fun with *listen and learn*.

The End

Story No. 10

Live and Let Live

Billy Wild was a lot like his name—Wild!

His mom was often seen in the neighborhood, calling his name or chasing him down.

He liked being noisy.

He liked wrecking things.

Like the time he made a homemade slingshot out of a stick and big elastic band.

Stacking cans and shooting them down with pebbles shot from the homemade slingshot was his idea of fun.

Fun, till old man Doherty's window got broken!

Yeah, Billy was wild but fun!

"Hey, you guys, look over here," Billy yelled.

Several boys and girls from the block ran to see what was up.

Billy had found a red anthill that was huge. The ants were marching in and out of their home with military-like precision.

"Look at that big sucker!"

An oversized red ant was carrying a stick one hundred times his size.

"Wow! He's strong!" Ruth, the local tomboy, piped up.

Billy reached in his pocket and pulled out a small firecracker. "I say we blow 'em all away."

"Yeah, yeah," the group of children yelled. "Let's do it!"

Ruth looked sad. "*No … stop … stop*," she cried out. Everyone turned to look at her.

"*Why?*" Billy snapped.

"Because they're alive! That's murder. *Live and let live*!"

"You weirdo!" Gus spit out. "They're only ants! They don't count."

Billy looked down thoughtfully. He had a soft spot in his heart for Ruth. "Yeah, Ruth," he said. "These buggers bite. That's why they call 'um fire ants. What's so special about 'em, anyways?"

"Look, Billy." Ruth pointed with her finger. "Look at how hard they're working to build their homes. I bet that big one is a granddaddy or something. How'd you like to get blown to pieces just minding your own business? *Live and let them live*, please, Billy?"

Gus shoved Ruth aside. "Get lost, kid."

Billy jumped up. "Hey, take it easy, Gus. She's only a girl!"

"Take it easy, Billy. Hey, I got better things to do than play with you babies and a bunch of ants!"

The large group of children drifted away till only Billy and Ruth were standing over the anthill

"Look, Billy, the granddaddy ant is stuck behind that rock," cried Ruth.

"Okay … okay."

Billy bent down and removed the quarter-sized rock to allow the ant to pass.

"Thanks, Billy," Ruth said.

"Yeah, okay, kid. I know *live and let live*!"

"You're the greatest, Billy." Ruth smiled as she followed Billy down the broken sidewalk toward home.

The End

Story No. 11

One Day at a Time

"*Daddy, what day is it today?*" the golden-haired Meagan asked.

"Sweetheart, it's Wednesday, April 5," he answered in his deep voice.

"Is it my birthday yet?"

"No, not today. Four more days then it will be your birthday. *One day at a time*, Meagan."

"But, Daddy, I can't wait four days. It's too long!"

"We can't change time, Meagan. I know it's hard, but it won't be that long. Trust me."

"Okay … okay … but tell me again about my party," she asked.

"Well, let's see," he said as he reached down to lift his daughter up onto his lap. "There will be presents and a birthday cake and games, and your friends will be there too."

"Who's coming, Daddy?"

"Your aunts, uncles, cousins, grandma, and your friends—
Jane, Ruth, Martha, Isabel, and Tami. How old will you be,
Meagan?"

She showcd him five fingers.

"That's right! Let's count."

"One-two-three-four-five!" they counted.

The next morning, Meagan awoke with a start. *It must be
today!* she thought as she ran down the steps to the kitchen.

"Daddy, Daddy, it's time right for my birthday?" she
yelled loudly.

Meagan's father laughed. "No, sorry, pumpkin. Three more days."

"Oh no!" she cried in disappointment

"Oh yes!" her father answered.

"You know, Meagan, that's just how your mom and I felt when we had to wait for you to be born. You were one whole week late! But Mom reminded me, *one day at a time*. We had to wait for you, Meagan."

"I'm sorry I was late, Daddy. Were you mad?"

"No, we weren't mad, just excited. But we had to wait *one day at a time* for *God* to send you to us."

Meagan stared down at the floor. "I know I gotta wait too!"

"That's right, sweetheart. *One day at a time*!"

Finally, Sunday came. It was a bright, beautiful spring day.

"Rise and shine, birthday girl!" she heard her father calling. "Rise and shine!"

Meagan bolted from her bed and screamed in delight, "Is it my birthday, Daddy?"

"Yes, pumpkin, it sure is! Happy Birthday. You made it *one day at a time*, Meagan. You are really five years old today."

Meagan smiled. "Tomorrow, I'll be five years and one day old!"

"Remember, every day is special when you live *one day at a time*, Meagan."

The End

Story No. 12

Think

"You stink!" Melissa cried.

"Yeah, well, you double stink!" Emily yelled back.

"You're not my friend anyway," Melissa snapped back.

"I don't want to be your friend anymore anyway," Emily answered.

The two girls stood staring at each other.

Just then Melissa's mom popped her head out the screen door.

"Girls, girls, what's all the yelling about?"

Both children started talking and pointing at one another at once.

"Slow down, you two. Slow down and *think*! Now, you first, Emily."

"Melissa said I stink, and she won't play right! I'm supposed to get my turn on the swing and she wouldn't let me. Then she pushed me!"

"*Liar, liar*, hope your tongue catches fire!" Melissa screamed.

"Melissa, *stop*! What's your side of the story, Melissa?"

"Emily took her turn for too long, then acted like a cry baby when I took my turn. She stinks!"

"Melissa and Emily! I'm surprised at both of you. You are supposed to be friends. Friends take turns and don't call each other bad names. That hurts! *Think* before you speak. Words can hurt."

Both girls' eyes filled up with tears.

"You know, a glass of lemonade and some cookies might help you both to *think* more clearly. What do you say? Come on … let's all say we're sorry and start over."

Both girls nodded.

As they sat at the kitchen table in silence, sipping their cool drinks and munching on cookies, they peeked at one another.

"Girls, time to make up," the mom said soothingly.

Emily broke her vanilla wafer and handed half to her pal Melissa.

Both girls smiled.

"So, girls, next time you want to call someone a name. Stop and *think!* Promise?"

"We promise," they sang out.

The End

Remember, be a buddy not a bully!

Suggested Passages for Bible Reading

Story No. 1 - John 15:4

Story No. 2 - Luke 6:20

Sermon on the Mount - Matthew 5:3-7:27

Story No. 3 - Luke 4:4

Story No. 4 - John 12:36

Story No. 5 - John 14:18

Story No. 6 - Mark 10:27

Story No. 7 - Matthew 7:7

Story No. 8 - Luke 6:28

Story No. 9 - Mark 8:17

Story No. 10 - Matthew 7:12

Story No. 11 - Matthew 6:34

Story No. 12 - John 7:16

The Nugget Series:
Portion of proceeds to go to recovery programs for families.

About the Author

Growing up with deaf-mute parents made Florence especially sensitive to visual learning. Mary and George, her parents, acted out their stories in sign language. Or in her mom's case, dancing in the kitchen with flowing scarves. They handed Florence small books about Jesus that Ruth, her sister, would read to her. The impact of these moments molded Florence's brain in a healthy and imaginative way. Later in life, she pursued nursing as a career at two community hospitals and also spent sixteen years at Massachusetts General Hospital Boston, Massachusetts, in neurology and women's health. That experience led to a clinical pastoral course through the chaplaincy department that deepened her relationship to *God*. Presently, Florence lives in Plymouth, Massachusetts, and has two daughters, four grandchildren, and two great-grandchildren. Florence continues happily to serve in the realm of pastoral nursing for her church, the Second Church of Christ, in Manomet, Massachusetts.

CPSIA information can be obtained
at www.ICGtesting.com
Printed in the USA
BVHW02s1751200818
524796BV00007B/32/P